THE
FINAL
DRIVE

WHAT YOU NEED TO WIN

DAVID HAYS

authorHOUSE®

AuthorHouse™
1663 Liberty Drive
Bloomington, IN 47403
www.authorhouse.com
Phone: 833-262-8899

Published by AuthorHouse 05/20/2021

ISBN: 978-1-6655-2534-3 (sc)
ISBN: 978-1-6655-2535-0 (e)

To my Mom, Rhea, who is the sweetest, kindest, and most loving person I know. As I wrote this book, I have watched her Dementia progress. She is beginning to forget memories and common things are becoming difficult for her. Regardless, her sweet nature continues to shine through.

I love you Mom.

CONTENTS

ACKNOWLEDGMENTS

I would like to thank my family for always being supportive and dedicated to each other. My wife Misti and my son Will, who give me purpose.

Thank you to my mom, Rhea, and my dad, Jerry. Thank you to my step-parents John and Jeanne, who have been in our lives for the past 35 years. To all my siblings, who have always had each other's back, and who I can call for anything at any time and they will be there.

Special thank you to the Boys and Girls Club, for giving us a place to hang out and play basketball and football.

To my youth football Coach Mike Hoffman, who was dedicated for years coaching the youth of our community. To my football coach in Middle School, Chuck Jones, who always made football fun and was so supportive of me when I moved schools my 8th grade year. To John Chance, who wasn't just a Coach at Edgewood High School, but a friend. To coach Ron Beatty for showing confidence in me, as a Sophomore, to put me in the Game. To Ralph Haynes who coached us my Senior year, putting a new offense in and sticking with his Senior to lead our team.

To all my friends who truly believe in iron sharping iron, and keeping each other accountable. I don't know what my life would be like without such a strong "friend group". A special thanks to Ed Slott for helping keep me educated on important tax issues.

Thank you to Bunger and Robertson for giving me a job and allowing me to be around professional people.

To my office, from a one-man band in 1994 to an office of 15, with thousands of client relationships, thank you for your loyalty and your love for our business and our clients. We are truly blessed to be in this industry.

FOREWORD

BY ED SLOTT, CPA

Taxes will be the single biggest factor that separates you from your retirement dreams. As David Hays aptly points out in the pages that follow, you may only have one chance to land safely in retirement, and this book is the first step.

The goal is to win the retirement game by keeping more of your hard-earned savings and paying less to the IRS. But that takes planning and a team of professionals who have specialized knowledge in retirement tax planning. That's where you're in luck. When it comes to educated advisors, David Hays is one of the first names that comes to my mind. In my 30 plus-year career of training financial advisors to help people achieve financial security in retirement, I have rarely seen any advisor more committed to continually building his expertise by attending workshops, seminars, and conferences all over the country. For over the 20 years I have known Dave he has had a voracious appetite to learn all he can to help his clients be better prepared for their retirement years; especially when it comes to protecting their IRAs and 401(k)s from what could be excessive and confiscatory taxes yet to come, just when you'll need the money most - in retirement, when the paychecks stop, and the taxes begin.

Most financial advisors (more like 99%) do not have the level of advanced planning knowledge that Dave has in helping you win the retirement game by playing in the second half, when you take your money out. The average financial advisor can help you accumulate and invest for your retirement, but when it comes to IRAs and 401(k)s, it's what you keep that counts – *after* taxes. You can't spend money that you fork over to Uncle Sam. Keeping more though requires specialized retirement tax planning, but that is where David Hays shines.

David realized this early on in his career. He and I met because, as an educator I was also on a mission to help people learn how to protect and grow their retirement savings with tax planning strategies. Dave was one of the first advisors in the entire nation to rush aboard when I first launched *Ed Slott's Elite IRA Advisor Group*[SM], the nation's leading source of advanced IRA distribution training for financial advisors. He and a small handful of other advisors who also knew that this was the way to provide the highest level of retirement planning advice to their clients were the first members (our *Charter Members*) and almost 20 years later, David is still there at our workshops and virtual training sessions soaking up all he can to share with you. He is also generous about sharing his knowledge with other financial advisors.

Learn from the years of experience and knowledge David has gained and shared with you here. He correctly addresses the ominous cloud of higher taxes looming, but also shows you what you can do now to fight back by "riding at the dog" and "packing your parachute" (You'll have to read on to find out what that means!).

I am so proud and honored to write this book foreword because I know firsthand that David values education and helping people protect their retirement savings. You'll need a team of specialists for this, and with Dave as your coach – the fix is in. He offers gems of advice here. He shows you how to play offense (and defense) to have more, keep more, and make it last – and most of all to sleep at night with peace of mind knowing you have a ringer on your retirement team – the Peyton Manning of retirement tax planning!

-Ed Slott, CPA and Retirement Expert
Author and founder of www.irahelp.com
Founder of Ed Slott's Elite IRA Advisor Group^{SM}
March 31, 2021

PREFACE

2025, The Final Drive is a metaphor of my football playing and coaching days. In an attempt to emphasize the importance of: the last chance, time is ticking, and now is the time to go!

As you read through this book you will see we have a real opportunity in front of us. In 2025 the current tax cuts that we passed in 2017 will expire and we, at a minimum, return to the rates before or rates can go much higher.

With trillions of dollars in retirement accounts across this country, Baby Boomers retiring in droves, your retirement is at a real risk of being decimated by higher taxes coming. We have deferred taxes in our retirement accounts for decades and it will catch up with us. When should you pay the tax on your retirement accounts? At the farthest point in the future or when rates are the cheapest? If you answered, when rates are the cheapest, then read on. If you think otherwise put this book down now, pull your window shade down, and pretend nothing is happening.

The Congressional Budget Office, a non-patrician department of the government, has said over the past decade that taxes must double for us to simply pay for the things promised and to keep America from going bankrupt.

I don't know about you, but that gets me wondering what can I do to protect what I have, protect my family and my future.

In this book I will discuss the big 3 retirement risks and how to deal with them. Getting out of the way of higher taxes is #1, retiring into a bad market is #2, and pulling it together with the biggest risk of all, Longevity Risk is #3.

Longevity Risk isn't just about living too long, longevity is a risk multiplier. The longer you live a lot can go right, but a lot can go wrong. From higher taxes decimating your retirement accounts, to inflation eroding your purchasing power, the chances of another market crash destroying your savings; or long-term care taking everything you've saved. All I'm saying is, a lot can happen in a 40-year retirement "plan".

So, take your time, soak in the information you're about to read, and act! My goal has always been to inspire the people we touch to do the right things financially. I was put on this path at a young age and continue this path as I move into my 50's and beyond. Thank you to my Mentors, Coaches, Teachers, Family and Office Staff, for helping me along the way; my appreciation is beyond words.

God Bless You and God Bless America! Read on…

David Hays

CHAPTER 1

WHY IS THIS SO IMPORTANT?

WHEN I WAS 11, I wanted so badly to go on a trip to Kings Island amusement park as part of a class trip – the price covered our lunch, tickets to get in, and a little spending money. It cost $25, and that was the issue.

Let me set the stage for you: My mom was 17 when she had my older brother, Dan, and by the time she was 26, there were 4 of us, she was divorced, and unemployed. We lived with our Grandma and Grandpa, where my Grandma ran an in-home daycare and Grandpa was a Bloomington firefighter. So, when I asked mom if we had $25 for me to go, my mom's standard answer was: "No, honey, I'm sorry. We're broke."

Mom never talked to us about money, but that was probably because she never knew she should. She's worked hard her entire life, taking jobs at RCA and GE as a factory worker, and then getting laid off. We relied on food stamps and free lunches at school, and let's not forget that yummy government cheese! Even outside of our home, it was a rough economic landscape at a national level in the 70s and early 80s.

We may have been poor in funds, but we were fortunate enough to be rich in family and love. So that I could take advantage of the trip being offered, my dad took me to Fulk Wholesale, where I bought a wholesale-sized box of Blow-Pops to sell and make enough money to go on the trip with my friends. Grandpa Hays gave me the $10 to buy the box of Blow Pops, and I was off on my first entrepreneurial adventure.

I sold the pops at Grandview Elementary on the playground, that probably cost about a nickel apiece, for a quarter. I made $35, paid my Grandpa back and went to Kings Island. Many years later, sitting at lunch with my dad, someone asked us about this story.

"When did you know David would be successful?"

My dad responded, "I knew he would be successful after seeing him work so hard to make that trip happen".

I have a wonderful legacy from my family here in Monroe County, Indiana. I am a fifth-generation local boy. My mother's side of the family farmed, what is now Cascade Park for several generations, and my Great-Grandfather on my Dad's side founded the bustling downtown Hays Market in Bloomington, In. He was a sharp businessman, who was extremely generous and kind, and unfortunately passed when I was very young. Even though I didn't get to know him, being a fifth-generation member of the family, he left a long-standing legacy behind that helped shape the path I found myself forging later in life.

I really believe my drive and confidence began when I was 8 years old. My mom signed me up for football through the Boys Club, and I landed on a team called the Patriots. Because of the team I was on, my teammates, and my coach; this is what shaped me to who I am today. After that first year as a running back wearing number 42, my coach, Mike Hoffman, pulled me aside and told me he wanted me to be

quarterback. I was so excited; I could hardly believe he had picked me for such an important role on the team. Me, a kid living with Grandma and Grandpa on food stamps and free lunches was going to be a team leader and key player; so my jersey number changed to 14.

A little bit on Mike. He was a cool dude. He was a doctor, he drove a Cadillac, dressed nicely and had a big Burt Reynolds type mustache. Mike was the type of guy, if you asked me, I wanted to be when I grew up. I wanted to be like Mike.

Here's the thing, it turned out I was pretty good at football. We even won the "Superbowl" that year; and still today have lifelong friends from that team. Once I entered junior high school, where the players from various elementaries merged, I earned the position of quarterback at Batchelor Middle School and was catapulted into a new role as one of the most popular kids in school. Meanwhile, still on food stamps and free lunches. I still remember my free lunch number I had to give while going through the cafeteria line at Batchelor: number 126.

Going into my eighth-grade year, my mom got re-married to my awesome stepdad John; whom she's still with today. I had to relocate schools from Bachelor to Edgewood, where I stayed throughout my high school years. At that point, our family was lucky enough to find more financial stability. John worked at GE and my mom had been working at Cook Inc, a large medical device company in our home town. We were finally able to get off the free lunches and we no longer needed food stamps.

I played hard. And not just at ball.

By high school, my love of football only increased and I changed my jersey number from 14 to 10. In my young mind I felt like the number 10 was the best. If you were a "10" you were the best! Strait-laced and self-demanding, I was someone my coach could count on to lead my fellow players by example. I never partied and was just focused on winning. For example: it was understood that to stay focused, players should steer clear of their girlfriends on game days to keep their mind focused on the game that night.

I played hard and expected my teammates to do the same, and they did. "You're not a quitter," I reminded a teammate who told me he was quitting the team one day at school, and he kept trying. Many years later, I ran into that teammate who reminded me of that interaction, and he said it was a pivotal moment for him. One thing my teammates knew about me was that I hated to lose and I cared about them. My competitive spirit only increased with age, being voted All Conference and Most Valuable Player of my high school team.

By the time I was ready to graduate high school, I had decided my future career would be a Math Teacher and Football Coach – I loved numbers, and football was obviously my other passion, so it seemed a natural combination to me. But my high school football coach, Ralph Haynes who was our new coach my Senior year, had become one of my mentors. He encouraged me to think outside this particular box. "Go on to college, get what experience you can, and if you want, you can always come back here and coach with me," he would say. So that's what I did.

In the years that followed, my success, passion, and overall love of football (especially as quarterback) just grew and grew. After graduating high school, I was lucky enough to get a chance to play college football at Greenville College. Following the advice of my high school football coach, I took the offer and went off to Illinois where I joined the Greenville Panthers, trading my number 10 (because it was taken) back to the old Boys Club Patriot jersey number 14.

At Greenville I wasn't put on the traveling squad right away, so while the team traveled to the away games, I had weekends free, and wanted to use the time productively. There had been this TV commercial running about a personal finance and investment guru, Charles J. Givens, who was offering a weekend seminar on "Debt and Cash Flow Management." It's hard to explain, but something inside drew me to register and attend the seminar. They were talking about money, I didn't have any, so I made the trip to St. Louis to see what it was all about. After attending, it was like I had found my calling, I was hooked!

Putting it into practice, I came back bursting with advice for my mom. Suddenly, I was talking to her about refinancing to reduce her mortgage, saving money for retirement, investing, and life insurance. At the time something that was a fairly new topic of conversation. Bless her heart, she played along, and I'd like to think that in the long run it really benefitted her. I still have all the cassette tapes, binders, and books from that series of lessons from 30 years ago.

I realized that year what I was here to do in life: Help people make good decisions about their money. How to make it, how to save it, how to keep it, and how to best spend it in retirement.

Suddenly, I found that business school was going to have to be next on the agenda. After two years at Greenville, I transferred to Indiana University, where I studied accounting and finance while I lived at home with my dad.

CHARLES J. GIVENS
Financial Library
Audio Tapes & Reference Manual
Charles J. Givens Organization 1988

While in college I found myself navigating my way through a series of jobs and training programs. An entrepreneur at heart, I found myself running a driveway sealcoating business. I even turned my Ford Escort into a work vehicle. I took the passenger seat out of it to stow the buckets of tar and brushes, and when it was not used for blacktop sealing, I would put a lawn chair in as the passenger seat.

Another idea that came to me while working as a courier for a local law firm, was a same-day local delivery courier service after noticing how many business people asked me to "drop off" letters or paper to other offices. I called it the Local Mail Business Couriers.

I got married in October of 1993 to my wife, Misti, and finished at Indiana in December. Not long after, I was hired by the New England Financial Group and made my way to Boston for my first official training as a financial advisor. We moved out of my Dad's house and pulled my investment posters off the wall. While most guys my age would have music groups or beer posters, I had an investment poster explaining a complicated investment strategy. I still remember Misti looking at them and asking, "What in the world is 'bearish or bullish?'"

My beautiful wife, Misti, chuckles when asked about our early days. As I was just starting in my professional career, she finished beauty school with a regular clientele. Her long-term ambition was to go to LA and be stylist for the stars, but I convinced her to trust me. We were going to make it right here in our hometown, and she did.

In the years I spent building my business, Comprehensive Financial Consultants, things were still pretty tight for us financially. I had a word processing typewriter in a little office in downtown Bloomington, specifically in the old Grand Plaza building. Misti was actually my first assistant, part time while she continued as the breadwinner doing hair. She'll be the first to admit she knew nothing about the business and really had no interest in it whatsoever. She put up with me for a while, but one day she came in and explained, "We can either be married, or I can be your assistant, but not both."

During those early years, we lived in Heatherwood Trailer Park and you might say my unofficial motto was "fake it 'til you make it." Putting it plainly, I was very aware of image and appearances. If Misti said, "Let's make a trip to WalMart", I'd say, "Ok, but I need to take a shower and get dressed up first." Even for WalMart I preferred to look pretty business-y in case I came upon any current or potential connections.

Back in 1994 my firm consisted of a small office with a couch, a typewriter, and a copy machine. Initially, I started out by setting appointments with people I knew among my circle of friends and their families, and eventually branching out as I received more referrals. These were what you might call 10-minute "Dog and Pony" shows, during which I'd illustrate where a potential client might be financially and where they might want to go in the future. All while discussing different strategies we could use to get them there.

In the summer of 2003, we moved into our current location in Bloomington with about 5 employees and around $30M under management. Fast forward, and that tiny operation has now grown into a team of 15 employees serving thousands of clients. Now we have over a half a billion and that's been entrusted to our management and supervision. We're proudly growing and trying to make a difference in our community. Through it all, our mission has remained the same:

to inspire the people we touch to do the right things finically for themselves, their families and their business. We will educate and communicate giving them confidence in our abilities to serve them.

Let me step back a bit. My dad was always a great support. We would spend every other weekend at his house and six weeks in the summer. Some of my fondest memories were those long summers at Dad's riding bikes, playing "front yard" football, fishing, and tons of other things I probably shouldn't admit too! He had his own struggles finding his life path like many others during this time; he worked in my grandfather's restaurant and tried his hand at real estate sales. He eventually ended up with a job at the Workingmen's Federal Savings and Loan as an Assistant Loan Officer, where he worked work his way up through honesty, hard work, care for others, and his love for Christ, family, co-workers, and customers.

Like many in their generation, my mom and dad moved through their working years without much advice on what they should be doing to prepare for retirement. Those were the years when everyone had pensions waiting for them after years of loyalty to an employer such as RCA or GE. All you had to do was put in the years, be a certain age, and you were in good shape with guaranteed income for life.

McCORMICK'S CREEK PARK

Dad with his boys

You've maybe heard of the three-legged stool of retirement. A pension was one leg, Social Security the second, and personal savings was the third. These days there are almost no pensions and the Social Security leg is wobbling a bit. That leaves personal savings. That once-sturdy stool is looking a bit like a pogo stick!

What you'll see now is that we're in a YOYO world: "You're on Your Own." And most of us could use some coaching to make the best of our earnings.

My life took off on a long path the day my coach asked me, at 8 years old, to be the team quarterback. Because of that team, the coaches I had growing up, my family, and my friends; the opportunities opened up for me, and I followed them. I found a calling and have continued to follow that call.

During those early years Misti and I raised a son, Will, who was a wrestler at Bloomington South and singing and performing in "Sounds of Sound", their advanced choir. He is currently finding his own way, while studying at IU Purdue University in Indianapolis.

We believe in being a business that is generous to its community, and we support the Boys and Girls Club, the Monroe County Court Appointed Special Advocates (CASA) for Children, Big Brothers Big Sisters, and the Children's Organ Transplant Association; among many other charitable local organizations.

My passion for coaching people about money is as strong now as it was back in the days when I was fresh out of Charles J. Givens' seminar, calling my mom to give her the benefit of my newfound learning.

In addition to my work with clients at my business, I teach classes in financial management at Ivy Tech Community College. I have a weekly radio show and podcast, "Your Money, With David Hays," about current financial events and financial planning strategies, and am a co-author of Today's Guide to Retirement Planning.

And, yes, I'm coaching football! My hope is to have the same kind of influence on the kids my coach, Mike Hoffman, had on me so many years ago right here in my community.

In 2018 I had a kid on my team, I'll call him Billy. The first day of practice he came running up to me, with his oversized pads flapping in the wind, and said, "I want to be a receiver!"

What Billy didn't know that at 8 or 9 years old, it's not common to pass the ball that often. As Woody Hayes once said, when you throw the ball, three things can happen and two are bad. One you can catch it and the other two things… well it's bad. Nonetheless I said, "Billy, I'll give you a chance to be a receiver", and he turned out to be a good one. Fortunately for Billy there was another little boy that could throw the ball, so we would have a passing game! We won the Championship that year and Billy caught a touchdown pass in a championship game that helped us win. I can guarantee he will never forget that. I didn't know until halfway through the year that Billy was in foster care and football was all he had. My hope is that maybe, just maybe, Billy looks back as I have and says, "Because of the team I was on, and the coach that I had, it has set me on a path to where I am today"; "Coach Hays believed in me".

So here I am, hoping to inspire you to do the right things financially for yourself, your family, and your business. I want you to feel confident in the financial decisions you make. I'm hoping to educate you on the key things, you need to know, to have a successful financial life and win!

CHAPTER 2

THE EYE OF THE STORM

2020 WAS A CRAZY YEAR, the COVID-19 pandemic swept the world, putting fear into people everywhere. First the NCAA cancelled March Madness, the NBA season was played in a "Bubble," and much of college football was played without fans. We wore masks to slow the spread of the virus, then we were told they may not actually protect you, but maybe protect others from you. Schools closed, businesses were shuttered, we wiped down boxes delivered to our doors, avoided family gatherings, but continued to shop at big box stores while being told we shouldn't go into a restaurant, get your haircut, or go to church.

Everything was getting cancelled out of confusion, frustration, and fear of what might happen next. It was obvious the world made a choice of health and human safety over the economy. In an attempt to avoid a complete collapse of our economy, the government passed bill after bill, and spent trillions and trillions of dollars to keep us afloat.

Anyone who took even a passing glance at the financial news from the kitchen counter TV learned something else: America was deeply in debt and, even worse, it was getting deeper in debt at a faster pace than at any year in our nation's history. At the beginning of 2020 our country was already well over $22 trillion in debt, and planning to run a trillion-dollar deficit (which means we planned to spend a trillion more that year than is brought in from tax revenue).

To this add an unprecedented $3.2 trillion stimulus package that was passed, as I wrote this book, Congress passed another $1.2 trillion stimulus package. Now we are in a real mess as we approach $30 trillion in debt and adding more every year. Financially finding ourselves huddled up together, trying to figure out what play to call next, and realize we are in "The Eye of the Storm."

"Eye of the storm" is a metaphor for a quiet place in a time of frenzy. Just like the quite time I would spend with my football teammates before we called the next play, knowing it was one of our last chances to get the lead before the game was over. Quiet reflection in those moments brings about awareness. Awareness leads to strategy. Strategy leads to tactics, which leads to action and execution – finally brings about results. It all begins here – in the eye of the storm.

What is a Trillion?

Most people have no idea what a million dollars represents, let alone a trillion. So how much, truly, is a trillion dollars? Try this example that I borrowed from economist Tom Hegna: If one dollar equals one second, a million dollars equals 11½ days, a billion dollars equals 32 years, and a trillion dollars is 32,000 years! Our government already owes 30 times that, and it's growing by another 32,000 years with every passing year.

Simply put, this is not sustainable. Here's another example: If you took a trillion dollars in $100 dollar bills and stacked them straight up, you would be stacking money 8 miles higher than the International Space Station!

Here is the math behind the debt problem: Currently over 91 cents of every dollar of all tax revenue coming into to the US is paying for four things: Medicare, Medicaid, Social Security and interest on our debt, leaving 9 cents to pay for everything else.

How is this sustainable? Simple answer, it's not. However, some would question this thought, since it has been going on for decades, without any meaningful consequences.

Riding at the Dog

You've probably heard about taking the bull by the horns, but you've probably not heard about riding at the dog. When I was a around 8 years old, my younger brother, Mark, and I would ride our bikes to the Monroe County Fair during the last days of summer. We'd ride down Harmony Road, across the highway, and then turn right up Garrison Chapel Road. Each day we would stop at the bottom of the hill on Garrison Chapel next to this old house on our way up that hill.

This is one of those long-graded hills, so it took all we had to make it to the top. At the top of the hill, we always knew, there was this big mean dog that would chase after us. This was the only route to the fair, so we had no choice but to ride past that house where that mean dog lived so we could turn right on Airport Road, and coast into the fairgrounds. We tried to sneak by, we tried to ride fast, but we could never avoid the hill or the dog. Obviously, it was worth the risk, we loved to go to the fair and walk around with our friends, but we always knew we had that one major hurdle to get over, the DOG!

After three days of being chased and pinned down by this snarling and barking out of control dog, I told my brother, "When I get to the top of the hill, I'm going to ride straight at that dog, and you ride as fast as you can past the house, and then I'll try to ride through." I knew there was no ditch between the road and the yard so aiming for the dog would not involve any major rocks, ditches, or trees that would cause me to crash. Besides, what did I have to lose?

We got to the top of the hill and I rode hard at that dog as fast as I could go. I was shrieking, screaming, yelling, even barking at him, as fast as I could go, hard at that dog. The dog stood there staring at me growling and snarling, but what happened next sets up our story. That dog was afraid of me. It turned on its heels and ran away!

For the next three days, until the end of the fair, when we got to the crest of the hill I would ride at the dog, not away from it, and we safely made it to the fairgrounds. Why do I tell you this story? Because this is your chance to ride at the dog. We can ride at the problem that is in front of us or we can keep riding like we have been, hoping we don't get chased or bitten down the road.

But the fact is that you will get bitten, there is really no question about it. I'm talking about getting bitten by high taxes! I'm going to show you how to avoid the storm of higher taxes coming our way by calling the right plays, directly from my playbook, for you to use in your personal huddle.

Those IRAs and 401ks

We Americans have been putting money away tax deferred, (which means you'll pay the tax when you take it out) for decades in our 401ks and IRAs. Believing we will be in a lower tax bracket when we retire. If everything stays as it is now, that's a good argument, but we know mathematically things can't stay the same and that's why it's so important to understand what is in front of us: a challenge that can be largely muted if the right steps are taken now.

We can all avoid higher taxes destined to decimate our retirement accounts in the future at an unknown rate, and in the not-too-distant future. We can do it by pedaling right at the tax problem right now. Face the problem head-on and cash in at these historically low and known tax rates. There is no point to waiting to see what the future holds. It's virtually an immutable, mathematically fact: taxes are going to go up!

The Case for Why Taxes Will Go Up

Our government is in serious need of money. And, chances are, government strategists are looking closely at your retirement savings to get that money. They know exactly how much you had in your retirement savings accounts a year ago and how much that has been growing over the past several years. Have you ever seen a tax document sent to you in or around May, Form 5498? It is a report to the IRS to tell them exactly how much you have in your IRAs. Your 401k provider must provide details on how much is in your company 401k retirement accounts.

It's been well known, for decades, millions of people have been putting away trillions of dollars in their tax deferred retirement savings; expecting to pay the tax when they pull it out and expecting to be in a lower tax bracket.

What you need to understand is, everyone planning for retirement by saving money in their IRAs and 401ks has a silent partner: the IRS. And in this case, the silent partner is calling all the shots too by setting tax rates, collecting those taxes, telling you how much, and when you must start taking money. Eventually, that partner is going to step in and take its share. Count on it.

Can you imagine getting into a partnership where you put in all the capital and all the hard work, but you have a partner who expects a share? That really does describe your retirement accounts. You've put it all in, maybe your employer matched, but even your employer doesn't say "I would like my share back when you retire." It's yours. Right now, we know the percentage of ownership that partner — the IRS — has in our retirement accounts. It could be as low as 10 percent or as high as 37 percent — but who knows what it will be in the future. We all have a choice: pay them off now or take the gamble of what future tax rates will be.

The Congressional Budget Office says taxes need to double to simply pay for the promises we've already made. To add to that, they come out every year with new estimates and they're not getting any better. Should you take the deal that's in front of you, or roll the dice and hope for a better deal from that silent partner, the IRS? Of course, this is a rhetorical question, clearly you should take the deal!

Other Solutions?

Now you know the money in your retirement account is looking more and more like part of the solution to one of our country's greatest problems – the deficit and the debt. You might ask, how else can our country find money to pay its debt? Obvious answers are to cut spending, raise taxes, or a combination of both.

Any householder would agree that reducing spending is a way to balance a budget overrun, but for the government it's not so simple. The people doing the would-be cutting are elected officials who owe their jobs to the voters who might think spending cuts are fine in general, but not cuts that may affect their own lives such as closing a local military base.

The cuts could also come from benefits programs such as Social Security or Medicare, but here again, politicians face serious challenges from voters over such sensitive proposals. This isn't new news, in fact the Wall Street Journal has printed numerous articles on the topic of deficits, debt, and spending. In July of 2019 it ran an article titled "Federal borrowing soars as deficit fears fade." An article in March of 2018 reads "State budgets face historic squeeze." In that article the US Secretary of Health and Human Services projected that Medicaid costs alone are growing so fast that within 10 years it could "crowd out virtually every other category of spending." Higher education, infrastructure, and safety, would all get squeezed out.

Bottom line, it's just easier to raise taxes than to try to cut spending, as history has shown us time and time again.

Taxes Are Going Up – How High?

If you have any doubts about whether or how high taxes can go, take a look at the history of our tax code, it's been nothing short of a rollercoaster ride.

Income taxes as we know them today were first collected in 1913. At the time, it was supposedly temporary, and the top rate was 7 percent. Those rates have fluctuated widely over the last century, rising to more than 90 percent for the top earners in times of crises such as World War II.

Focusing on the top rate has been common, but what about the lower income tax rates? In the 1960s, the lowest rate was 20 percent (twice what the lowest rate is today) and the highest was 91 percent (two and a half times higher than today)!

Marginal Tax Rates in the United States

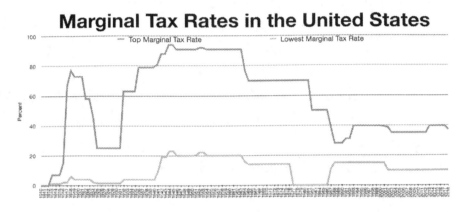

Photo Credit: Yahoo Finance

I have a copy of my mom's taxes from 1973. She worked in a factory at RCA, she had three young boys at home with combined income of $16,000. After a standard deduction and exemptions, their taxable income was $13,500. Did they owe income taxes, making those few dollars with that many dependents, surely not? The answer is yes! In fact, they paid over $2,600 in federal income taxes, or 20 percent!

If you don't believe taxes can double, simply take a look into the past and you can see that we have been there before. To quote philosopher George Santayana, "Those who cannot remember the past are condemned to repeat it"

Form 1040

US Individual Income Tax Return — Department of the Treasury—Internal Revenue Service — **1973**

For this year January 1–December 31, 1973, or other taxable year beginning .... 1973, ending .... 19....

Name (If joint return, give first names and initials of both) / Last name: RHEA J. ▓▓▓▓

Present home address (Number and street, including apartment number, or rural route): 1616 OAKDALE EAST

City, town or post office, State and ZIP code: BLOOMINGTON INDIANA 47401

COUNTY OF RESIDENCE: MONROE

Your social security number: ▓▓▓▓
Spouse's social security no.: ▓▓▓▓

Occupation — Yours ► ENGINEER — Spouse's ► ASSEMBLY

Filing Status—check only one:

1. ☐ Single
2. ☒ Married filing joint return (even if only one had income)
3. ☐ Married filing separately. If spouse is also filing give spouse's social security number in designated space above and enter full name here ►
4. ☐ Unmarried Head of Household
5. ☐ Widow(er) with dependent child (Year spouse died ► 19)

Exemptions — Regular / 65 or over / Blind

6a. Yourself — ☒ ☐ ☐
b. Spouse — ☒ ☐ ☐
Enter number of boxes checked ► 2

c. First names of your dependent children who lived with you ....

d. Number of other dependents (from line 27) ►
7. Total exemptions claimed ► 2

8. Presidential Election Campaign Fund.—Check ☐ if you wish to designate $1 of your taxes for this fund. If joint return, check ☐ if spouse wishes to designate $1. Note: This will not increase your tax or reduce your refund. See note below.

Income

9	Wages, salaries, tips, and other employee compensation. (Attach Forms W-2. If unavailable, attach explanation.)	9	▓▓▓
10a	Dividends (See instructions on page 6.) $............ 10b Less exclusion $............ Balance ►	10c	
10d	(Gross amount received, if different from line 10a .... $............)		
11	Interest income	11	10 —
12	Income other than wages, dividends, and interest (from line 38)	12	
13	Total (add lines 9, 10c, 11, and 12)	13	16969
14	Adjustments to income (such as "sick pay," moving expenses, etc. from line 43)	14	
15	Subtract line 14 from line 13 (adjusted gross income)	15	16969 —

- If you do not itemize deductions and line 15 is under $10,000, find tax in Tables and enter on line 16.
- If you itemize deductions or line 15 is $10,000 or more, go to line 44 to figure tax.
- CAUTION. If you have unearned income and can be claimed as a dependent on your parent's return, check here ► ☐ and see instructions on page 7.

Tax, Payments and Credits

16	Tax, check if from: ☐ Tax Tables 1–12 ☒ Tax Rate Schedule X, Y, or Z ☐ Schedule D ☐ Schedule G ☐ Form 4726 OR ☐ Form 4972	16	2627 25
17	Total credits (from line 54)	17	
18	Income tax (subtract line 17 from line 16)	18	2627 25
19	Other taxes (from line 61)	19	
20	Total (add lines 18 and 19)	20	2627 25
21a	Total Federal income tax withheld (attach Forms W-2 or W-2P to front)	21a	3308 51
b	1973 estimated tax payments (include amount allowed as credit from 1972 return)	b	
c	Amount paid with Form 4868, Application for Automatic Extension of Time to File U.S. Individual Income Tax Return	c	
d	Other payments (from line 65)	d	6 62
22	Total (add lines 21a, b, c, and d)	22	3315 13

Balance Due or Refund

23	If line 20 is larger than line 22, enter BALANCE DUE IRS ► (Check here ► ☐, if Form 2210, Form 2210F, or statement is attached. See instructions on page 8.) Pay in full with return. Make check or money order payable to Internal Revenue Service	23	
24	If line 22 is larger than line 20, enter amount OVERPAID	24	687 88
25	Amount of line 24 to be REFUNDED TO YOU ►	25	687 88
26	Amount of line 24 to be credited on 1974 estimated tax. ►	26	

Note: 1972 Presidential Election Campaign Fund Designation.—Check ☐ if you did not designate $1 of your taxes on your 1972 return, but now wish to do so. If joint return, check ☐ if spouse did not designate on 1972 return but now wishes to do so.

Sign here

Under penalties... including accompanying schedules and statements, and to the best of my knowledge and belief it is true...

Signature: ▓▓▓▓ 2/26/74

Preparer's signature (other than taxpayer): ▓▓▓ BLOCK DPI 072 2/14/74

44 — 0607856

Spouse's signature (if filing jointly, BOTH must sign even if only one had income)

Address (and ZIP Code): ▓▓▓

Another example of how things can change is the Social Security payments for workers and employers is when the benefits program was enacted in the 1930s.

Promises made by big government can't always be kept. Notice the line where it says "That is the most you will ever pay". You are the most reliable guarantor of your retirement investments and plans.

SECURITY IN YOUR OLD AGE

SOCIAL SECURITY BOARD
Washington, D. C.

To Employees of Industrial and Business Establishments

FACTORIES • SHOPS • MINES • MILLS • STORES
OFFICES AND OTHER PLACES OF BUSINESS

TAXES

THE same law that provides these old-age benefits for you and other workers, sets up certain new taxes to be paid to the United States Government. These taxes are collected by the Bureau of Internal Revenue of the U. S. Treasury Department, and inquiries concerning them should be addressed to that bureau. The law also creates an "Old-Age Reserve Account" in the United States Treasury, and Congress is authorized to put into this reserve account each year enough money to provide for the monthly payments you and other workers are to receive when you are 65.

YOUR PART OF THE TAX

The taxes called for in this law will be paid both by your employer and by you. For the next 3 years you will pay maybe 15 cents a week, maybe 25 cents a week, maybe 30 cents or more, according to what you earn. That is to say, during the next 3 years, beginning January 1, 1937, you will pay 1 cent for every dollar you earn, and at the same time your employer will pay 1 cent for every dollar you earn, up to $3,000 a year. Twenty-six million other workers and their employers will be paying at the same time.

After the first 3 years—that is to say, beginning in 1940—you will pay, and your employer will pay, 1½ cents for each dollar you earn, up to $3,000 a year. This will be the tax for 3 years, and then, beginning in 1943, you will pay 2 cents, and so will your employer, for every dollar you earn for the next 3 years. After that, you and your employer will each pay half a cent more for 3 years, and finally, beginning in 1949, twelve years from now, you and your employer will each pay 3 cents on each dollar you earn, up to $3,000 a year. That is the most you will ever pay.

YOUR EMPLOYER'S PART OF THE TAX

The Government will collect both of these taxes from your employer. Your part of the tax will be taken out of your pay. The Government will collect from your employer an equal amount out of his own funds.

This will go on just the same if you go to work for another employer, so long as you work in a factory, shop, mine, mill, office, store, or other such place of business. (Wages earned in employment as farm workers, domestic workers in private homes, Government workers, and on a few other kinds of jobs are not subject to this tax.)

Photo Credit: Social Security Office

What About Other Taxes?

Taxes have long been used in the US to encourage behaviors, such as Dependent Exemptions and Child Tax Credits to encourage family creation, mortgage interest deductions to encourage home ownership, or deductions for charitable giving to encourage generosity. Taxes have been used to discourage behaviors as well, such as taxes on alcohol and tobacco. What's next? Fast food, sugary drinks, processed foods? It's all been attempted in the past, so it's possible.

What are other possible tax increases? A national sales tax? Increased gas taxes? (This could encourage electric cars.) Taxes on cell phone usage? Could there be a tax on the buildup of cash value in life insurance, or the elimination of stepped-up cost basis on appreciated assets at death? Currently if you own an appreciated asset, like land, and you pass away, your heirs inherit this at its current value. If sold at that appreciated amount, they would pay no tax; this is called "stepped up cost basis."

What about the federal estate tax as another area to increase revenues? When I started in 1994 the federal estate exclusion amount was $600,000. Which meant any part of your estate larger than that amount was subject to a tax, as much as 55 percent! In my 26-year career, I've seen the exclusion amount go from $600,000 to $1 million, $2 million, to $10 million, then go away completely in 2010 (the year NY Yankee's owner George Steinbrenner passed away), and then come back to $1 million the very next year! Heading into 2017 it was a little over $5 million, but was doubled to $11 million, only to sunset back to $5 million in 2026.

Are your IRAs and 401ks also subject to the federal estate tax in addition income taxes? The short answer is yes, with some deductions of taxes paid to offset some of the carnage.

Payroll tax is another tax that will likely go up, it really has to. If you're employed, your employer pays half and you pay half. The total is 15.3 percent of your pay goes to pay for current Medicare and Social Security recipients. With the Social Security Trust Fund scheduled to be out of money in a little over 10 years and Medicare practically already there; payroll taxes must go up.

The good news for retirees is that the money coming out of retirement accounts is not subject to payroll taxes. That's good news for the retirees, bad news for their workings kids and grandkids who are paying the tab. But in terms of overall gain, the biggest target under government crosshairs is the money in retirement accounts that will come out as income as the Baby Boomers start to hit their 60s and 70s and draw from these accounts. This is literally the only tax that we have any chance of managing.

Like I mentioned earlier, you and millions of others like you, have been saving a percentage of your earnings in tax deferred investments like IRAs or 401ks. It was a sweet deal: You could put the money in, receive a tax deduction now, defer the tax on your growth, let it grow, and maybe pay less in taxes when the time came to spend it. Don't feel bad, we all bought the narrative, but that hope of a lower tax rate is expiring... literally. In 2017 the government enacted the Tax Cuts Jobs Creation Act that cut income taxes, and these lower tax rates expire after Dec. 31, 2025.

So, something we can call a fact, is that taxes will go up beginning in 2026. It was written into law that rates would automatically revert, at a minimum, to where they were prior to the tax cuts being enacted.

In the next chapter we'll dive into that playbook I mentioned earlier with real strategies to help you shelter your retirement account from higher taxes coming and accumulate more money tax free.

We are in the eye of a fiscal storm, we know exactly when the storm will hit, and now is the time to prepare. Doing this isn't easy emotionally until you recognize the issue, believe it's true, and become super focused on the solution. You can deal with the problem at hand (ride at the dog), or stay home, and pull down your window shade like there is no storm coming.

By paying much of the tax owed on your retirement accounts, the IRS will thank you now, and you and your family will thank you later. Read on!

CHAPTER 3

GETTING PREPARED: PLAY OFFENSE

T O FULLY TAKE ADVANTAGE OF these historically low tax rates it's important to understand the taxation system.

First: we live in a "marginal" tax system. Which means we live in a next-dollar system of taxation. For instance, you either take the standard deduction or you itemize. Then and only then do you step into the tax brackets. The first level of income after deductions is taxed at 10 percent, the next at 12 percent, then 22 percent, 24 percent, 32 percent, 35 percent, and finally 37 percent.

Married Filing Jointly Brackets - 2021

Taxable Income	Ordinary Income Brackets
0 - $19,900	10%
$19,900 - $81,050	12% (was 15%)
$81,050 - $171,750	22% (was 25%)
$171,750 - $329,850	24% (was 28%)
$329,850 - $418,850	32% (was 33%)
$418,850 - $628,300	35% (Same)
$628,300 +	37% (was 39.6%)

Photo Credit: White Glove Workshops

Married Filing Brackets for 2021

I love to do this exercise in front of a group of people:

Looking at these tax brackets, if you currently have taxable income of $81,050 (right at the edge of the 12 percent bracket) and you received a $10 raise, which puts you into the 22 percent bracket, would that materially change your tax situation?

In a large group, I have most nodding their heads yes, but the answer is no! It's only that next $10 that is taxed at the 22 percent rate, not everything. Are you starting to get an understanding of why it's so important to know where you are in your tax bracket? It's for planning purposes. Leaving a portion of a tax bracket on the table is like a gift card expiring at the end of the year. If you didn't use it up, you lose it. We've shown you the 2021 tax brackets above for married people filing joint returns, but what does the tax bracket look like if you're single? Well, nearly everything is cut in half: your deductions, your brackets, everything.

Single Filing Brackets - 2021

Taxable Income	Ordinary Income Brackets
0 - $9,950	10%
$9,950 - $40,525	12% (was 15%)
$40,525- $86,375	22% (was 25%)
$86,375 - $164,925	24% (was 28%)
$164,925 - $209,425	32% (was 33%)
$209,425 - $523,600	35% (Same)
$523,600 +	37% (was 39.6%)

Photo Credit: White Glove Workshops

Single Brackets for 2021

One of the main reasons we preach moving money from taxed later to tax free is because, even if you're married, at some point you will likely be filing a tax return as a single person. Not necessarily because of divorce, although that's possible, but because of death. At the death of the first spouse a couple of things happen, and they're both bad. You lose income (the smallest Social Security check goes away, and maybe part of a pension) and your taxes double. So, at the time you might need more money, you're paying twice as much in income taxes than you did before.

The Roth Conversion Game Strategy

Once you figure out where you fall in the tax brackets, determine how much you can convert from your traditional retirement accounts to a Roth IRA, within that bracket, and whether it makes sense to move on into the next bracket.

Be cautious. The extra income may cause "side effects" or some unintended consequences. What are some of these "side effects" or unintended consequences of extra reportable income, besides paying more federal and potentially state tax? If you are Medicare age, it could cause you to pay much higher Medicare premiums. If your income exceeds $200,000 filing as a single individual or $250,000 filing married jointly individuals, then you could pay an additional 3.8 percent tax on all investment income, which includes capital gains and dividends, interest and annuity payments, and passive business income (like rental properties). Always be aware of the cause and effect of having extra reportable income.

That's why having a professional help you with this analysis is important.

What is a Roth?

A Roth IRA, 401K or 403B is a retirement savings vehicle that allows you to pay the tax on the contributions, or conversions. The accounts grow tax deferred, and when distributed, the money comes out tax free to yourself or your beneficiaries.

I always ask an audience: if you were a farmer and you had the choice of paying taxes on the seed you put in the ground or the harvest it creates, which would it be? Unanimously, the answer is the seed not the harvest. This is a Roth IRA. You pay tax on the money that goes into your account, never to pay tax again!

I wouldn't put one cent away without paying the tax now. In other words, if I have the choice, I would put 100 percent of my money away into the Roth. It might be a Roth IRA, Roth 401K or 403B, it doesn't matter; pay the tax now at a known rate to never pay it again.

My dad is in banking and let's pretend you go see him for a loan. When you ask him what the interest rate is, he says "Don't worry about it, we'll let you know when we need your money." Who would sign up for that? But that's exactly what you are doing when you put your money away tax deferred. You are delaying the tax and taking the chance that when you do take it out, taxes are much higher than they are today.

If you are participating in a 401K, it's likely you are receiving a matching contribution. The matching contribution is going into the "taxed later" bucket, so even if you put all of your money away into the Roth, you will have plenty of money to pay the tax on later.

Now what about converting? Taking money that is in the "taxed later" side of the equation and moving it over to the "never taxed again" side of the equation, this is called a Roth conversion.

Most 401K plans that offer a Roth option also offer "in-plan Roth conversions." This means you can ask your retirement plan provider to convert funds from the "taxed later" side to the "never taxed again" side. When you do a conversion, you will need to set aside the funds to pay the tax. Ask your HR Advisor to increase the tax withholdings from your paycheck, or use whatever refund you are expecting, to pay the tax.

You can't have the tax withheld on a conversion in a 401K, but you can on an IRA conversion. However, if you are under age 59½ and ask for tax withholdings on a Roth conversion, those withholdings would be considered an early distribution and you would likely be subject to a 10 percent early distribution penalty. If you are over 59½, you could have the taxes withheld, but that's less money in your Roth to grow tax free. So, anytime you do a conversion, regardless of your age, I would suggest you pay the tax with money outside of your IRA.

When is the best time to do a conversion? Well obviously, before we get to the end of 2025 when the current tax code expires, but during the final drive between now and 2025 you can be very strategic about your conversion.

I like to use this philosophy: if the stock market declines by 10 percent or more than do your conversion, or before the end of that year, whichever comes first. Why on a correction? Well, if the market drops (which happens frequently) you can move your investments over at lower prices and when it recovers (which it always has) you benefit from that rebound all tax free.

In the Spring of 2020, the stock market fell over 30 percent from February 19 to March 24. During that time, we were converting IRAs as fast as we could. Did we know the bottom was there? No, but we knew we were more than 10 percent down and it was time to go. The great news is what normally takes over two years to recover happened in a few months and our client's Roth IRAs reaped the benefits of the rebound and it came back all tax free!

Another opportunity that arose from the Pandemic of 2020 and the loss of revenue for so many businesses was using their net operating losses to recognize more income from their IRAs. A friend of mine runs a sandwich shop that was closed for three months, then reopened to 30 percent capacity and lost about $100,000 in 2020. Thankfully, he applied for the Paycheck Protection Program and had some savings to get him through; but nonetheless, he lost $100,000 in his business. As they say in politics, never let a good crisis go to waste, but I would say never let a good net operating loss go to waste. My friend was able to covert $100,000 of his IRA to a Roth, use his business loss to offset the income and move his money from "taxed later" to "never taxed again," tax free!

Another overlooked opportunity to put money away into a Roth IRA for non-working spouses. If you have a non-working spouse, you can make a contribution for them into a Roth each year (assuming your income doesn't exceed certain levels or your participation in a retirement account at work).

Another awesome opportunity to put money into a Roth is what is referred to as the "backdoor" method. Anyone, regardless of income, can make a non-deductible IRA contribution. Anyone, regardless of income, can convert an IRA to a Roth IRA. So, the technique is to make a non-deductible IRA contribution and then immediately convert it to a Roth. No gain on the IRA, no tax to be paid on the conversion. Beware if you have other IRAs. The IRS looks at all of your IRAs as one, so if you convert a non-deductible IRA it will include your other IRAs into the calculation to determine what gains must be taxed.

Here's an example: Let's assume you have a $50,000 traditional IRA and you want to do a "backdoor" Roth of $5,000. When you make the non-deductible contribution that $5,000 represents 10 percent of all your IRAs, so when you convert it, you will pay tax on 90 percent of the $5,000 converted. A way around this would be to rollover your IRA into your 401K and eliminate all other IRA balances, so you can do this "backdoor" Roth without any unintended tax liability.

Even if you have an IRA and you can't make sense of the "backdoor" Roth, you can always make a non-deductible IRA contribution and begin building a "basis" in your retirement account. Building a basis means you have already paid tax on part of your retirement, so when you begin withdrawing money in retirement the portion you already paid taxes on comes out tax free; only the portion you haven't paid taxes on, is taxable.

You must keep track of this basis on your annual tax filings, because the custodians reporting your distributions have no idea you have a basis in your IRA. This is also important to your heirs. If they inherit your retirement account, they have 10 years to recognize the income and pay the tax. If they don't know you had a basis in the retirement account, they would likely pay the tax on all of their distributions. Always check the tax return of someone who you inherit an IRA from, you never know if they would have had a basis or not.

Other Strategies

As you read this you may be thinking "I have to move all of my IRA to a Roth," but hold on for a moment. There is a right amount to keep in your IRA that isn't in a Roth — and that's for charitable giving.

Even though as I wrote this book, you aren't required to begin taking distributions from your traditional IRAs and 401Ks until age 72, you can begin giving money away from your IRA tax free to charity as early as 70½. This is called a Qualified Charitable Distribution or QCD for short. You can give up to $100,000 from your IRA annually to a charity, this distribution is non-taxable and if you are over 72, it goes towards any minimum distribution requirements as well. So, let's say you give $6,000 a year on average to your church and other charities. You might want to keep around $120,000 to $150,000 in your IRA for the purpose of charitable giving.

I normally suggest as a rule approximately 5 percent of your annual giving be left in your IRA. As an example, if you give $5,000 away to charity, you need to keep $100,000 in your IRA. You will not be able to deduct your contribution, but it's always better for it not to be included in your income at all. Plus in 2018 only 14 percent of taxpayers itemized and the rest used the increased standard deduction instead.

Other ideas on minimizing tax include gifting appreciated stock to a charity or to a Donor Advised Fund. I had a client who received a large deferred compensation distribution, and to offset some of his income he donated highly appreciated stock to his Donor Advised fund. He received a tax deduction for his contribution and avoided paying tax on the appreciated stock. He plans to do all of his giving later in life from this fund as opposed from his retirement income.

Lastly there are so many ways to avoid paying tax, live life to its fullest, and be incredibly generous along the way. I'm thinking about charitable remainder trusts, where you can give money away now, enjoy an income stream for your entire life, and receive tax benefits along the way. Using life insurance to provide a tax-free legacy for your family, while providing a long-term care benefit along the way.

This book isn't meant to solve all the world's problems, or all of your problems, but it is meant to emphasize the importance of working with a professional who knows these things. The pillars you build through a good relationship with a professional are: confidence and trust and someone you can rely on.

CHAPTER 4

THE BLITZ IS ON

Although I truly believe higher taxes decimating your retirement accounts is a monster risk you face, it is one that you can manage using ideas laid out in the previous chapter.

When playing quarterback, you are always looking for the "blitz". It's when a linebacker or defensive back comes at you out of nowhere. You have to be ready for it, just in case it happens and pick it up. If a blitzing linebacker isn't picked up, it's likely you're caught off guard and sacked for a loss.

The blitz I'm referring to financially, is the biggest risk of all, something known as longevity risk, the "great risk multiplier." What do I mean by a "risk multiplier"? It's a risk that brings on the possibilities and probabilities of new risks.

For example, when I go to visit my son in Indianapolis, my assumed risk is that I could be in an accident on my way. How do I manage this risk? I drive the speed limit, keep a lookout for other drivers doing crazy things, and don't slam on my brakes when I stop. There are several things I can do to manage my risk driving to Indianapolis. However, the more I drive to see him, the more likelihood I could be in an accident at some point. The more often I visit, the chances increase that I will have a flat tire, or some other mechanical issue that could hamper my trip or endanger myself or others around me. I can manage all of that known risk. But at some point, my car will get older and to the point that no matter how well I've maintained it, I shouldn't make the trip to Indy.

When it comes to life and finances, this great "risk multiplier" is called "Longevity Risk." You might think isn't Longevity Risk simply the risk of living too long? Who doesn't want to live a long healthy life? I think most people equate Longevity Risk to the risk of running out of money. That is the ultimate worry, but that's not the risk. The risk is what causes you to run out of money.

The first cause is withdrawal rate or sequence risk. This is the risk that may threaten even the most successfully planned retirement. This is when you assume a reasonable average rate of return, set withdrawals up accordingly, and still get left with too much retirement at the end of your money (sounds like a bad country song to me).

Let me show you what I mean. Look at the chart below. It shows your accumulation of money, using average returns, asset allocation and staying invested. In this example for simplicity, we show no withdrawals and a single upfront investment. Both Portfolio A & B begin with $100,000 at age 41, with an average return of 8 percent for both, no deposits, and no withdrawals. By the time the investor is age 65, they have the same amount of money, $684,848.

FACTORS AFFECTING PORTFOLIO RESULTS BEFORE RETIREMENT

Age	Annual Return (Portfolio A)	Portfolio A (Year-End Value)	Annual Return (Portfolio B)	Portfolio B (Year-End Value)
41	-12%	$87,695	29%	$129,491
42	-21%	$69,426	18%	$152,281
43	-14%	$59,707	25%	$189,590
44	22%	$72,984	-6%	$178,404
45	10%	$80,136	15%	$204,272
46	4%	$83,595	8%	$221,183
47	11%	$92,707	27%	$281,124
48	3%	$95,210	-2%	$274,939
49	-3%	$92,155	15%	$315,355
50	21%	$111,507	19%	$375,272
51	17%	$130,129	33%	$498,737
52	5%	$137,026	11%	$554,097
53	-10%	$123,597	-10%	$499,795
54	11%	$137,316	5%	$526,284
55	33%	$182,493	17%	$614,174
56	19%	$217,167	21%	$743,150
57	15%	$249,091	-3%	$719,305
58	-2%	$243,611	3%	$738,726
59	27%	$309,629	11%	$819,247
60	8%	$335,262	4%	$854,602
61	15%	$383,875	10%	$938,354
62	-6%	$361,226	22%	$1,147,022
63	25%	$449,727	-14%	$986,439
64	18%	$528,878	-21%	$780,941
65	29%	$684,848	-12%	$684,848
	8%	$684,848	8%	$684,848

Photo Credit: Guardian Life

Now this person has reached retirement and the focus must change from accumulation to the distribution phase. During this phase, how your returns occur (sequence), product and investment allocation, and portfolio protection are the new focus. I'm going to show you the exact same returns, in the exact same order they came during the accumulation phase, but with annual withdrawals coming out to spend in retirement.

We have an annual average rate of return of 8 percent, so we could surely take 5 percent adjusted for inflation and be just fine, right? Unfortunately, when it comes to the distribution phase, average returns don't matter, it's how and when your returns come.

The next chart shows where both portfolios begin with the same $684,848, the investors ended their savings careers with the exact same withdrawal rate. Why does Portfolio A run completely out of money in less than 17 years, while Portfolio B, by the time the investor is age 90, is sitting at over $2.6M in the accounts? It's because of the sequences of how the returns occured. Portfolio A retired into a bad market, losing money each of the first three years, while the bad returns in Portfolio B came at the end, creating a much different outcome.

Age	Annual Return (Portfolio A)	Portfolio A (Year-End Value)	Annual Return (Portfolio B)	Portfolio B (Year-End Value)
		FACTORS AFFECTING PORTFOLIO RESULTS AFTER RETIREMENT		
66	-12%	$566,337	29%	$852,571
67	-21%	$413,086	18%	$967,355
68	-14%	$318,927	25%	$1,168,029
69	22%	$352,432	-6%	$1,061,698
70	10%	$348,431	15%	$1,177,105
71	4%	$323,772	8%	$1,234,855
72	11%	$318,176	27%	$1,528,614
73	3%	$284,653	-2%	$1,452,871
74	-3%	$232,143	15%	$1,623,066
75	21%	$236,215	19%	$1,886,771
76	17%	$229,644	33%	$2,461,500
77	5%	$194,417	11%	$2,687,327
78	-10%	$126,543	-10%	$2,375,148
79	11%	$90,304	5%	$2,450,746
80	33%	$68,219	17%	$2,808,226
81	19%	$27,833	21%	$3,344,606
82	15%	$0	-3%	$3,182,338
83	-2%	$0	3%	$3,211,664
84	27%	$0	11%	$3,503,440
85	8%	$0	4%	$3,594,592
86	15%	$0	10%	$3,885,017
87	-6%	$0	22%	$4,685,257
88	25%	$0	-14%	$3,963,710
89	18%	$0	-21%	$3,070,398
90	29%	$0	-12%	$2,622,984
	8%	$0	8%	$2,622,984

Photo Credit: Guardian Life

Sequence Risk when you retire can make a big difference, see the chart below that demonstrates having $1,000,000, investing in a blended mix of stocks, bonds and cash with a withdraw rate that most Americans believe is sustainable. The difference between retiring in 1980. versus 1990 or versus 2000, when the market dropped three consecutive years (similar to the chart above), result in very different results.

Strategies for a sustainable income in retirement

Sequence risk - when you retire can make a big difference

Assumptions

- $1 million portfolio

- 5% withdrawn annually and increased each year to keep up with inflation

- Invested in a portfolio of 60% stocks, 30% bonds, and 10% cash

Portfolio balance remaining after 10 years of withdraws

$1,731,989 $1,861,592

$472,238

Retire in 1980   Retire in 1990   Retire in 2000

Photo Credit: Putnam Investments

The question I would be asking is how do I manage this risk; would it be the same way I managed my drives to Indianapolis to see my son? The answer is through proven techniques that are tested and work. Withdrawal strategies vary as much as the weather in Indiana, but to break it down let me tackle a few for you.

Income for Income

First is income for income and growth for growth. This is very difficult to use in a low interest rate world, but here is the concept:

I put enough money in contractual interest-bearing investments to provide my income, while putting the rest in growth to head off inflation and maintain purchasing power. If you want $50,000 a year from a $1,000,000 portfolio, this method does not work for you. As I write this book, high quality bond rates are below 3 percent, so even if you put all of your money in bonds, you would receive $30,000 per year at best, with no funds left to grow and hedge anything. You would need approximately $1,800,000 in fixed income to provide $50,000 per year of income. So, my suggestion without $2,000,000 and a $50,000 per year need, you should not consider this coveted method of retirement income planning.

The Buckets

The other method, which is preferred during times of low interest rates, is the "bucket method."

This is a design to invest money differently for different periods of your retirement, similar to the way Pension Fund managers invest their money for payout to their beneficiaries. Here's how it works: Let's say again you want $50,000 per year in income. We would set aside 10 to 15 years of income into investments that aren't affected by the stock market and distribute it to you as income; we will call this the "soon" bucket, that is, money we need sooner than later. Meanwhile. we leave the remainder of your money to grow, untouched, in the market for those 10-15 years, or the "later" bucket.

Looking back over rolling 15 year-periods in the stock market, assuming money is left untouched, the market has done quite well. Let's go back and assume you had $1,800,000 in retirement and you would like $50,000 per year in income. If we assume a 2 percent return on your "soon" bucket, you would need to allocate $648,000 of your $1,800,000, leaving $1,152,000 to grow. If your average return on over the next 15 years was 6 percent on this "later" bucket (far below the 30-year average of the market), your account would grow to $2,760,000; more than replacing what you started with in the beginning.

Annuitization

The last, and maybe the most underutilized, is the annuitization method of retirement income planning.

It is important to plan for a long time in retirement. In fact, the numbers suggest that if you and your spouse are both age 65, there is a 50 percent chance one of you will live to 92 and a 25 percent chance one of you will live to 97! This is where the annuitization method comes into play.

If you are planning for yourself and your spouse, you must plan like you will live into your 90s, but insurance companies don't. They assume you will live a "normal" life expectancy of 85 or 86, and this is where it gets good. When you use the annuitization method you are not just managing risk, but truly transferring your risk of running out of money to an insurance company. So, what can an insurance company do for you, when you can manage it for yourself? Any investment can give you your money back in retirement. Any investment can give you back interest or dividends, but only an insurance company can give you the third ingredient, which is a "Mortality Credit".

"Mortality Credit" it is the credit given to those who live longer than the average. The money from those who died earlier, pays for those who live longer. Here's an example I borrowed from economist Tom Hegna, author of Paychecks and Playchecks:

Four friends, all 90-year-old women, decided to pool their money and invest it together. Instead of buying the next hot stock or putting money into a CD, they decided to all put $100 each into a shoe box and leave it for a year to see what happened. The next year they all descended on the shoe box, but unfortunately one of the ladies had passed away, so there were only three of them. In her honor they decided to leave the $400 in the box and come back again next year. The next year came and sadly another one of the ladies had passed during the year, so now there were two. So, they open the box, split the money and wished each other well. So how did they do on their investment?

Emotions aside of losing two of their friends, pretty darn good. In fact, each of them made $100 or 100% on their investment over two years. This return came with no stock market, no bonds, no CDs, no gold or Bitcoins, but in the form of Mortality Credits. The two women received their credit, their returns, for simply living longer.

This is the secret sauce that only an insurance company can provide. The reason they can provide a Mortality Credit is that they are on both sides of things. If people are dying early, they are paying out life insurance claims, but no annuity payments. If people are living longer, less life insurance claims and more annuity payments. In fact, most large pension funds have transferred their pension liabilities to insurance companies. Transferring the risk away from the company books because, a pension fund is only on one side of it is the income side.

This brings me to the final thought on the "great risk multiplier," longevity risk.

The longer we live, a lot of things can go really right, but things can go really wrong, too. We have to plan for, the things that can go wrong. Market risk, withdraw rate and sequence risk, inflation, deflation, increasing taxes and long-term care summarize the components of longevity risk. This makes longevity risk hands down the number one risk in retirement. The longer you live the more likely the market will crash; the longer you live, the more likely you will withdraw too much money; the longer you live, the more likely inflation will decimate your purchasing power; the longer you live, the more likely you will need long-term care. To retire successfully, you must address all of these and do your best to take longevity risk off the table.

CHAPTER 5

THE FINAL DRIVE - IT TAKES A TEAM

IN THIS BOOK I'VE LAID out why being a financial advisor is so important to me and the importance of understand the urgency behind my message. Time is not on our side. We know, best case, that we will enjoy historically low tax rates until the end of 2025 before taxes, at a minimum, return to their previous higher levels and likely much higher.

Is it a coincidence that the amount of money in tax-differed 401ks and IRAs are almost identical to the amount of debt our country has accumulated? I'm sure it is, but we can't ignore the issue any longer and now is the time to act, hence the title of my book "2025 The Final Drive."

But First a Flashback

It's October of 1987, Homecoming. The stands are packed, cheerleaders yelling and we have the ball with time running out. We are down 6 points, with less than 4 minutes to play, I'm in the huddle with my teammates. We were playing Avon High School, from the west side of Indianapolis. Avon was really good and we were the obvious underdogs after only winning two games the previous year.

I remember heading into the huddle and saying with a smile on my face, "isn't this fun? Time is running out; your team is down and you must score." I told them: It's just like playing football in the front yard, pretending time is running out and you throw it deep to your brother or best friend, and they catch it for a touchdown. They jump up and down, do a dance, spike the ball and the feeling of winning is real.

So, I told them, let's just play and let's go win this thing. That's exactly what happened. We moved the ball down the field and with less than 20 seconds to play, we were on the 3-yard line. I noticed the defensive line had shifted and thought: opportunity! We didn't really have audibles (changing the play at the line of scrimmage before the snap), but we had instincts. I tapped Bill, our center, on the left leg, he nodded his head, I tapped my left guard on the butt and snapped the ball. I ran hard left, planting my foot in the turf, then right, diving into the end zone for the touchdown! I will never forget that moment, neither will my teammates.

What would I have done without a team around me? There's no way one person could take on 11 people and win. I tell you this to emphasize that everything I have talked about in this book isn't easy to do on your own, you need help. You need a professional, someone who understands what to do, how to do it and can help you along the way. Just like my teammates helped each other to win. I think it's important to have someone leading your team who has a passion for what they are doing, can inspire those around them to want to work hard and do the right things. And, oh, have fun while doing it!

Packing Your Parachute

I say this often in public events, so I will share it with you. I might ask, how many times will you retire? Most in the audience will answer, once. I normally come back with, yes, you retire once, we help people retire every day. Would you allow us to help – to help you retire, to help you achieve security for you and your loved ones, to help you negotiate the tangled world of retirement income planning, investments, insurance, estate planning and taxes? I then enjoy telling the story of Charlie Plumb.

Charlie was a US Navy jet pilot in Vietnam. His plane was destroyed by a surface-to-air missile after 75 missions. Plumb ejected and parachuted into the threatening jungle below, right into enemy hands. He was captured and spent six years in a communist Vietnamese prison. He survived the ordeal and now lectures on lessons learned from that experience.

The story by Charles Plumb, "Who Packs Your Parachute," is a strong and interesting true story that has been shared with many people over the years during lectures and leadership courses. Interesting enough, when I shared this story with listeners of my radio program, I received an email from someone who had served in an Airborne unit who had heard this story before.

He told me that Charlie Plumb starts off his story by saying, "…. I was a fighter pilot, and he was just a sailor." Plumb recounts that one day, when he and his wife were sitting in a restaurant, a man at another table came up and said, "You're Plumb! You flew jet fighters in Vietnam from the aircraft carrier Kitty Hawk. You were shot down!"

"How in the world did you know that?" asked Plumb.

"I packed your parachute," the man replied.

Plumb gasped in surprise and gratitude. The man pumped his hand and said, "I guess it worked!" Plumb assured him, "It sure did. If your chute hadn't worked, I wouldn't be here today."

Plumb couldn't sleep that night, thinking about that man. Plumb says, "I kept wondering what he might have looked like in a Navy uniform: a white hat, a bib in the back and bell-bottom trousers. I wonder how many times I might have seen him and not even said 'Good morning, how are you?' or anything, because, you see, I was a fighter pilot, and he was just a sailor."

Plumb thought of the man-hours the sailor had spent on a long wooden table in the bowels of the ship, carefully weaving the shrouds and folding the silks of each chute, holding in his hands every day, each time he nestled the folds of cloth one into another, each time he arranged the array of cords into the pack, every nuance of his job shaped the fate of someone he did not know.

Who's Packing Your Parachute?

Now, Plumb asks his audience, "Who's packing your parachute?"

Everyone has someone who provides what they need to make it through a world that at best is a challenge and at worst is a disaster waiting to happen. Plumb also points out that he needed many kinds of parachutes when his plane was shot down over enemy territory. He needed his physical parachute, his mental parachute, his emotional parachute, and his spiritual parachute. He called on all these supports before reaching safety.

Going to a Specialist

Misti and I got married at 23 and I was 30 when we had our one and only child, Will. A few years after Will was born, we decided to try to have another baby. We tried and tried (which in itself was fun, of course!), but no baby. Then one day I woke up and I was 40, then 41, 42. My wife said, "this isn't happening, so it's time for you to go see the vasectomy doctor."

So, what did I say? Did I say, nah, I can do this on my own? I've looked online, I've watched some YouTube videos, I even read a book like this on vasectomies. A little cut here, a little snip there, a bag of frozen peas, how hard could it be? I've got this! How crazy does that sounds?

When you're dealing with something that important, you go to a specialist, a urologist, and let them take care of it for you. Retirement is really no different, most likely you'll only do it once. Why not find someone who packs the retirement parachute every day? And that's exactly what we do, pack parachutes every day.

In this book, a playbook for how to pack a parachute, we have discussed the three major risks in retirement. We've talked about how to avoid losing our money to excessive taxes; having a strategy to manage withdrawal rate/sequence risk and not run out of money; and, based on math and science, how to address the single biggest risk of all, longevity risk. With the right planning, you can take these risks off the table during what should be for most the best years of an already productive and eventful life.

Do you really want to attempt this all on your own? Again, you do it once, my associates and I do it every single day. We fold parachutes, and we do it well.

This career that chose me has been very rewarding. It's allowed me to help thousands of people retire successfully and provided an excellent standard of living for my family. I look back at my humble beginnings with pride and gratefulness. I'm grateful that my Mom was able to successfully raise her kids and retire comfortably. A long way from counting those pop bottles under the sink as her emergency fund. My Dad at 73 is still working and going strong, allowing him to travel, spend time with family and really enjoy life.

Another lesson my Dad showed us when we were kids, is no matter how tough it gets, continue to give. When we were young, Dad was going through a tough transition point in his life. He sat us all down and said things were tight and we were going to be cutting back on things, which included birthdays and Christmas.

But he made it a point to tell us we aren't going to stop giving to the Church. He said that God will get us through this and the obedience he showed and showed us, pulled us through. He had envelopes on his dresser and would put 10% of his income into these envelopes each week and would put it in the tray as it passed. He showed us that when it comes to money, you can do three things with it. Spend it, save it or give it. He proved that those who give first will always have more money to spend and save.

After Misti and I were Married, we weren't as committed to attending Church as we had been growing up. Granted we were told to get up, take a shower and put on your nice clothes, we really had no choice. Misti grew up with her Mom attending Church on Wednesday nights, Sunday mornings and Sunday nights, so maybe staying home in our trailer on a Sunday morning was appealing in our early 20's. Eventually we began attending Clear Creek Christian Church, where we were married, and began donating on a regular basis, and we certainly wanted to raise our Son in the Church as well.

Going back to my Dad and his tithing. Even though things were tight for Misti and I at times, we wanted to give 10% of our income to the Church, so that's what we started to do. I was looking at the boxes that held the envelopes for people to grab, our name wasn't on one already because we were new to this. As I looked over the numbered boxes, it hit me. More than 15 years later after being on free lunches, it hit me, there it is, number 126. I grabbed the box, stared at it for a minute and tears started coming down my face. Misti said "what's wrong with you"? I said it's my free lunch number, 126, we're taking this box. It's been over 20 years since I grabbed that box and even though we can now give electronically, I still sit down at my breakfast table, pull out a check and place it into that envelope numbered 126. Then when the plate is passed, I place it in plate and remember what it was like then and where we are today, with gratefulness and gratitude. Hoping my Son is paying attention, like we paid attention when Dad sat us down for that talk.

I know you can have a great retirement and leave a legacy goodness, kindness and generosity. You can travel when you want to travel, relax when you want to relax and serve when you want to serve.

You can have a great retirement!

Printed in the United States
by Baker & Taylor Publisher Services